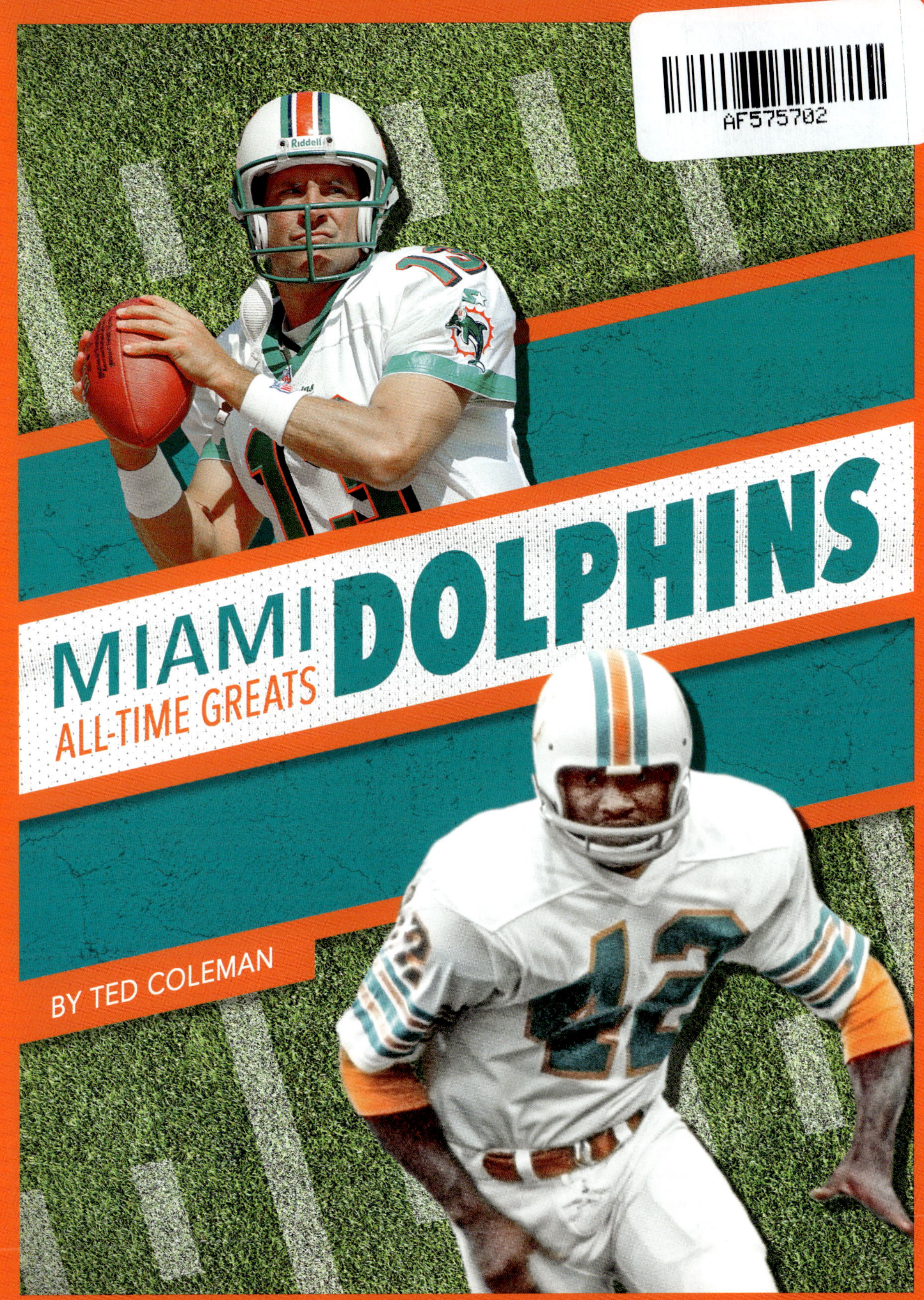

AF575702
MIAMI DOLPHINS
ALL-TIME GREATS
BY TED COLEMAN

Book design by Jake Slavik
Cover design by Jake Slavik

Photographs ©: G. Newman Lowrance/AP Image, cover (top), 1 (top); Al Messerschmidt/AP Images, cover (bottom), 1 (bottom); Focus on Sport/Getty Images, 4, 9; James Flores/Getty Images Sport/Getty Images, 6; Focus on Sport/Getty Images Sport Classic/Getty Images, 10; George Rose/Getty Images Sport/Getty Images, 13; Rick Stewart/Getty Images Sport/Getty Images, 15; Focus on Sport/Getty Images Sport/Getty Images, 16; Rick Stewart/Allsport/Getty Images Sport/Getty Images, 18; Eliot Schechter/Allsport/Getty Images Sport/Getty Images, 19; Doug Murray/AP Images, 21

Press Box Books, an imprint of Press Room Editions.

ISBN
978-1-63494-431-1 (library bound)
978-1-63494-448-9 (paperback)
978-1-63494-481-6 (epub)
978-1-63494-465-6 (hosted ebook)

Library of Congress Control Number: 2021916615

Distributed by North Star Editions, Inc.
2297 Waters Drive
Mendota Heights, MN 55120
www.northstareditions.com

Printed in the United States of America
012022

ABOUT THE AUTHOR

Ted Coleman is a sportswriter who lives in Louisville, Kentucky, with his trusty Affenpinscher, Chloe.

TABLE OF CONTENTS

GRIESE
12

CHAPTER 1
THE PERFECT SEASON

The Miami Dolphins began playing in 1966. For the first few seasons, fans had very little to cheer for. But in 1970, Miami got a new head coach. It didn't take long for Don Shula to lead the team to greatness. In the 1972 season, the Dolphins made National Football League (NFL) history. They became the first team to win the Super Bowl with an undefeated record. As of 2021, that record still hadn't been matched.

Quarterback **Bob Griese** played a big role in the team's success. Griese had always been a winner. In college, he led Purdue to its first

Rose Bowl victory. During his long career with the Dolphins, he won two Super Bowls.

Wide receiver **Paul Warfield** caught many of Griese's passes. Warfield spent only five seasons with the Dolphins. But in four of those seasons, he led the team in receiving yards. Warfield also hauled in 33 touchdown catches for Miami.

As good as Griese and Warfield were, the 1972 Dolphins were best known as a running team. They had three excellent backs. **Jim Kiick** never ran for big yards. But he was powerful. Kiick was at his best near the goal line. In the 1972 playoffs, he scored four touchdowns in three games.

Mercury Morris was a smaller back. Morris had great speed, and he ran for 1,000 yards in 1972. He also led the league with 12 touchdown runs.

Larry Csonka was another bruising runner. In the 1973 season, Csonka helped the Dolphins win their second Super Bowl in a row. He was named the game's Most Valuable Player (MVP).

DON SHULA

Don Shula coached the Baltimore Colts from 1963 to 1969. In 1970, he became the second head coach in Dolphins history. The team didn't hire another coach until 1996. Shula had only two losing seasons in his 26 years with Miami. He retired with two Super Bowl titles. He also had an NFL-record 328 career wins.

Miami also had a fearsome offensive line. The group was led by guard **Larry Little** and center **Jim Langer**. The duo played together for 10 seasons. Both players ended up in the Hall of Fame.

Miami's defense in the 1970s was known as the "No-Name Defense." They got that nickname because they didn't have any huge stars. Even so, they had plenty of great players. **Nick Buoniconti** was one of the best linebackers in the league. In the 1972 season, he had a key interception in the Super Bowl. It set up the game-winning touchdown.

Two great safeties played behind Buoniconti. In the 1972 season, **Jake Scott** was the MVP of the Super Bowl. He grabbed two interceptions in that game. Scott spent a total of six years with Miami. During that

time, he set a team record with 35 career interceptions. **Dick Anderson** was also a master at creating turnovers. He finished his career with 34 interceptions. He also recovered 16 fumbles.

MARINO
13

CHAPTER 2
AIRING IT OUT

In 1983, the Dolphins drafted quarterback **Dan Marino**. Miami instantly became a great passing offense. In his second year, Marino threw for 5,084 yards. He also tossed 48 touchdown passes. Both of those were NFL records at the time. Not surprisingly, Marino was named MVP. The Dolphins made it back to the Super Bowl that season. However, they fell to the San Francisco 49ers. Marino led the league in passing yards four more times during his career. When he retired, he was the NFL's all-time leader in more than 40 passing categories.

Marino had no shortage of great receivers to catch his passes. **Nat Moore** was already a veteran when Marino arrived. Moore spent his entire 13-year career with Miami. During that time, he caught 510 passes. He also scored 75 touchdowns.

Wide receiver **Mark Duper** joined the team in 1982. In 1983, he paired up with rookie receiver **Mark Clayton**. The duo soon became known as the "Marks Brothers." Both played for Miami through the 1992 season.

STAT SPOTLIGHT

CAREER TOUCHDOWN RECEPTIONS

DOLPHINS TEAM RECORD

Mark Clayton: 81

And both left their mark on the team's record book. Clayton ended up as Miami's all-time leader in receptions and touchdown catches. Duper set a team record for most receiving yards.

In the early 1980s, Miami's defense was known as the "Killer Bees." That's because several of the best players had last names starting with the letter B. Defensive end **Doug Betters** was one of the team's leaders. He was named Defensive Player of the Year in 1983.

Throughout the 1980s, Marino was protected by one of the best centers in the game. **Dwight Stephenson** started 107 straight games at one point in his career. He made the Pro Bowl five times in eight seasons.

In 1990, the Dolphins drafted **Richmond Webb**. Webb stood 6-foot-6 and weighed 325 pounds. The enormous left tackle protected Marino for a decade. During that time, he set a team offensive record by starting 118 games in a row.

WEBB
78

TAYLOR
99

CHAPTER 3

THE MODERN ERA

Most scouts didn't expect linebacker **Zach Thomas** to be a star. They thought he was too small and too slow. Even so, the Dolphins took a chance on Thomas. They selected him in the fifth round of the 1996 draft. The team figured Thomas would mainly play special teams. But he ended up making the Pro Bowl seven times. He recorded more than 1,600 tackles during his 12 years with the Dolphins.

In 1997, Miami drafted defensive end **Jason Taylor**. He went on to become one of the NFL's all-time sack leaders. But Taylor did

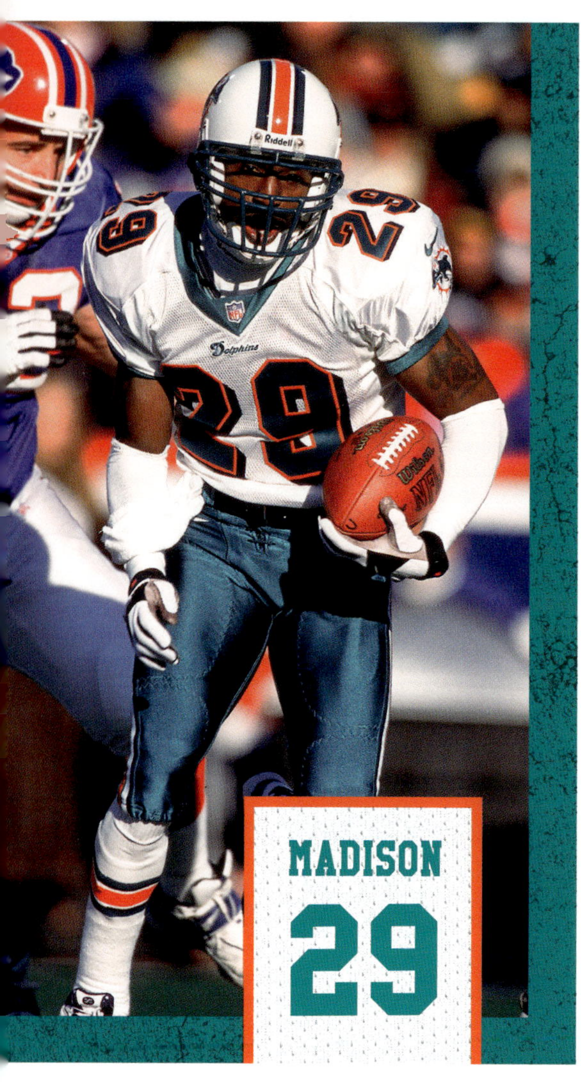

more than take down quarterbacks. He also forced 43 fumbles during his time with the Dolphins.

Miami's secondary was just as good as its defensive line. Cornerback **Sam Madison** made life tough for opposing receivers. He was named to the

STAT SPOTLIGHT

CAREER SACKS

DOLPHINS TEAM RECORD

Jason Taylor: 131

Pro Bowl four years in a row from 1999 to 2002. Madison finished his Dolphins career with 31 interceptions.

Cornerback **Patrick Surtain** spent seven seasons with Miami. And he made them count. Surtain grabbed 29 interceptions as a Dolphin. He also made the Pro Bowl three times.

Miami didn't have many offensive stars after Dan Marino retired. But one bright spot was running back **Ricky Williams**. He smashed the team's single-season rushing record in 2002. His 1,853 yards broke the old mark by nearly 600. Williams also scored a team-record 16 rushing touchdowns that season.

The Dolphins struggled for most of the 2000s and 2010s. However, they started to show signs of hope in 2020. The team won 10 games

THE WILDCAT

In week three of the 2008 season, Miami started using an unusual offensive formation. It was known as the wildcat. There was no quarterback on the field. Instead, running backs Ronnie Brown and Ricky Williams took snaps directly from the center. Confused defenses had a hard time stopping it. Thanks in large part to the wildcat offense, Miami won 11 games that season.

that season and just missed the playoffs. Cornerback **Xavien Howard** was one of the biggest reasons for the team's success. In his first five seasons, Howard led the league in interceptions twice. With players like Howard leading the way, Dolphins fans hoped it wouldn't be long before the team returned to glory.

TIMELINE

JIM KIICK
(1968–74)
1966
BOB GRIESE
(1967–80)
DICK ANDERSON
(1968–77)
LARRY CSONKA
(1968–74, 1979)
1970
MERCURY MORRIS
(1969–75)
LARRY LITTLE
(1969–80)
JAKE SCOTT
(1970–75)
NICK BUONICONTI
(1969–76)
1980
JIM LANGER
(1970–79)
PAUL WARFIELD
(1970–74)
NAT MOORE
(1974–86)
DOUG BETTERS
(1978–87)
DWIGHT STEPHENSON
(1980–87)
1990
MARK DUPER
(1982–92)
MARK CLAYTON
(1983–92)
DAN MARINO
(1983–99)
RICHMOND WEBB
(1990–2000)
2000
ZACH THOMAS
(1996–2007)
JASON TAYLOR
(1997–2007, 2009, 2011)
SAM MADISON
(1997–2005)
PATRICK SURTAIN
(1998–2004)
2010
RICKY WILLIAMS
(2002–03, 2005, 2007–10)
XAVIEN HOWARD
(2016–)
2020

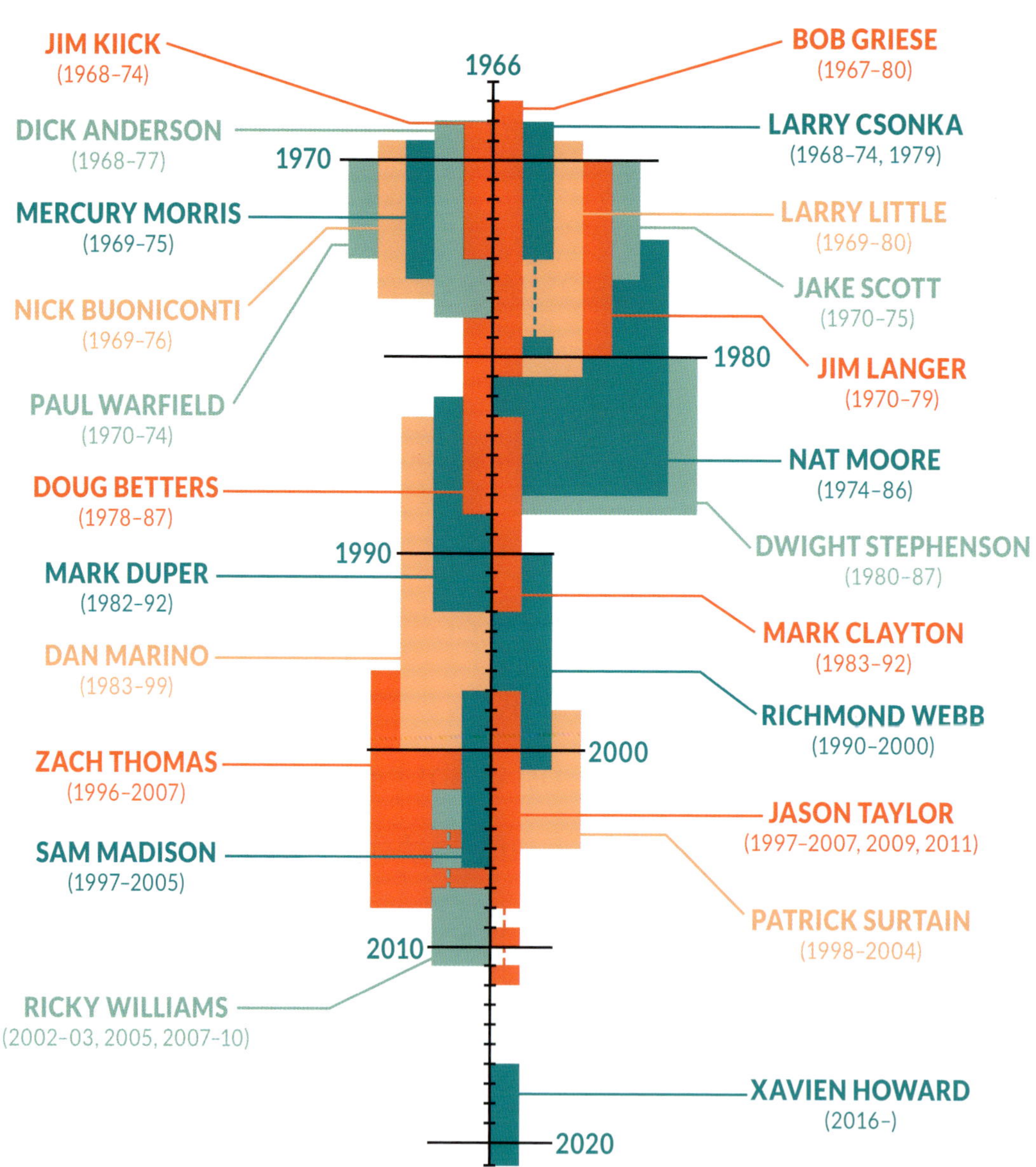

TEAM FACTS

MIAMI DOLPHINS

Founded: 1966

Super Bowl titles: 2 (1972, 1973)*

Key coaches:

Don Shula (1970–95), 257–133–2, 2 Super Bowl titles

Jimmy Johnson (1996–99), 36–28

Dave Wannstedt (2000–04), 42–31

MORE INFORMATION

To learn more about the Miami Dolphins, go to **pressboxbooks.com/AllAccess**.

These links are routinely monitored and updated to provide the most current information available.

**1966 through 2020*

GLOSSARY

draft
An event that allows teams to choose new players coming into the league.

goal line
The line that a player must cross with the ball to score a touchdown.

playoffs
A set of games to decide a league's champion.

scout
A person who looks for talented young players.

special teams
A group of players who handle kicks and punts.

turnover
Loss of the ball to the other team through an interception or fumble.

undefeated
Not having any losses.

veteran
A player who has spent several years in a league.

INDEX